Emperor Penguin

The World's Biggest Penguin

by Meish Goldish

Consultant: Heather Urquhart
Penguin Exhibit and Collection Manager
New England Aquarium
Boston, MA

BEARPORT
PUBLISHING

New York, New York

Credits

Cover © Leksele/Shutterstock; TOC, © Armin Rose/iStockphoto; 4, Kathrin Ayer; 5, © age fotostock/SuperStock; 6, © Corbis/SuperStock; 7, © Jan Will/Coldimages/iStockphoto; 8, © Bryan & Cherry Alexander/NHPA/Photoshot; 9, © Robert Harding Picture Library/SuperStock; 10L, © Flip Nicklin/Minden Pictures; 10R, © Daniel A Bedell/Animals Animals Enterprises; 11, © Bill Curtsinger/NGS Image Collection; 12, © Graham Robertson/Auscape/Minden Pictures; 13, © Cusp/ SuperStock; 14-15, © Biosphoto/Samuel Blanc/Peter Arnold Inc.; 16, © Gerald L. Kooyman/Animals Animals Enterprises; 17, © Biosphoto/Alain Torterotot/Peter Arnold Inc.; 18, © Fabrice Beauchene/Fotolia; 19, © Biosphoto/Antoine Dervaux/ Peter Arnold Inc.; 20, © Sue Flood/The Image Bank/Getty Images; 21, © David Tipling/NHPA/Photoshot; 22L, © Neale Cousland/Shutterstock; 22C, © Wayne Lynch/All Canada Photos/Alamy; 22R, © James Urbach/SuperStock; 23TL, © Biosphoto/Alain Torterotot/Peter Arnold Inc.; 23TR, © Frans Lanting/Corbis; 23BL, © Sue Flood/The Image Bank/Getty Images; 23BR, © Gentoo Multimedia Ltd./Shutterstock; 23BKG, © Jan Martin Will/Shutterstock.

Publisher: Kenn Goin
Senior Editor: Lisa Wiseman
Creative Director: Spencer Brinker
Original Design: Otto Carbajal
Photo Researcher: Picture Perfect Professionals, LLC

Library of Congress Cataloging-in-Publication Data

Goldish, Meish.
  Emperor penguin : the world's biggest penguin / by Meish Goldish.
    p. cm. — (More supersized!)
  Includes bibliographical references and index.
  ISBN-13: 978-1-936087-29-7 (library binding)
  ISBN-10: 1-936087-29-4 (library binding)
  1. Emperor penguin—Juvenile literature. I. Title.
  QL696.S473G65 2010
  598.47—dc22

                                    2009028108

For more information, write to Bearport Publishing Company, Inc., 101 Fifth Avenue, Suite 6R, New York, New York 10003. Printed in the United States of America in North Mankato, Minnesota.

102009
090309CGA

10 9 8 7 6 5 4 3 2 1

Contents

One Big Penguin

The emperor penguin is the biggest penguin in the world.

An adult emperor penguin is about as tall as a six-year-old child.

Both male and female adult emperor penguins can grow up to be about 40 inches (102 cm) tall. The males can weigh as much as 84 pounds (38 kg), while the females weigh about 65 pounds (29 kg).

5

Home on the Ice

Emperor penguins live in the coldest place on Earth—Antarctica.

Unlike some other types of animals, they don't build homes.

Instead, they live on top of the sea ice in the freezing, cold air.

The temperature in Antarctica can drop down to as low as −58°F (−50°C) in the winter. Winds up to 124 miles per hour (200 kph) make the air seem even colder.

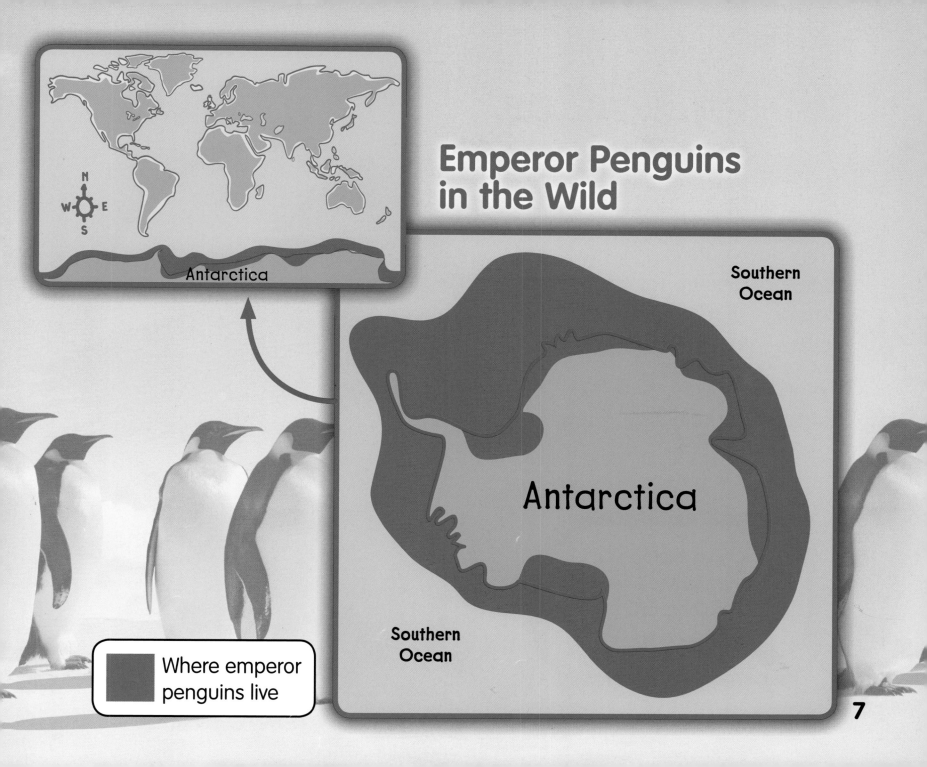

Emperor Penguins in the Wild

Antarctica

Southern Ocean

Southern Ocean

Antarctica

Where emperor penguins live

7

Warm Bodies

How are emperor penguins able to live in the very coldest weather?

They have a layer of waterproof feathers to keep their skin warm and dry while they swim in the cold water.

They also have a thick layer of fat to help them stay warm.

Every year, emperor penguins shed their old feathers and grow new ones.

feathers

9

In the Ocean

Emperor penguins are great swimmers.

They can dive as deep as 600 feet (183 m) into the ocean.

They swim very fast by moving their wings, which act like flippers.

It looks like they are flying underwater.

While they are swimming, they hunt for food, including fish, squid, and tiny animals called krill.

krill

Emperor penguins usually stay underwater for 3 to 5 minutes. Then they must come up to the surface for air. The longest dive ever recorded was 22 minutes.

wing

wing

A Long Walk

In April, emperor penguins leave the ocean to find a place to **mate**.

Thousands of them slowly march about 100 miles (161 km) away from the ocean.

They walk until they find a place on the ice that will not melt before their babies are born.

When they find a spot, the penguins break up into large groups, with each one settling in an area called a **rookery**.

Penguins walk, or **waddle**, very slowly. To move faster during their journey, they sometimes slide on their bellies, using their wings and feet to push them along.

Laying an Egg

In the rookery, male and female emperor penguins pair off to mate.

In mid-May, each female lays one egg, which she carefully rolls onto the feet of the male.

Then she walks all the way back to the ocean to get food for herself.

The mother will be gone for about two months.

When she returns she will also bring back food for her newly hatched baby, called a chick.

A male emperor penguin doesn't eat anything during the months he cares for the egg. He loses almost half of his body weight during that time.

15

Dads on Duty

While the female is away, the male keeps the egg on his feet, where it stays safe and warm under a fold of skin.

When freezing winds blow, all the males in the rookery stand close together in a **huddle**.

Those on the inside of the group get warm first.

Then they trade places with the penguins on the outside of the huddle.

No one stays cold for very long!

A penguin egg must be kept off the ice at all times, or the baby inside will freeze to death within a few minutes.

The Moms Return

In July, the chicks hatch from the eggs.

Right after they are born, the female emperor penguins return from the ocean.

Each mother feeds her new chick by spitting up food stored in her stomach into the baby's mouth.

The hungry males now make their way back to the ocean.

They need to eat and to get more food for their babies.

Emperor penguins locate their mates by calling to each other. Each pair of penguins has a special call.

On Their Own

At five months old, the young penguin is old enough to live on its own, so it heads to the ocean.

It knows how to swim, even without being taught!

In the water, the young penguin hunts for its own food and looks out for enemies such as leopard seals and sharks.

By age five or six, it will be old enough to start its own family.

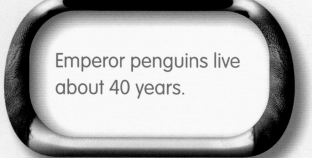

Emperor penguins live about 40 years.

More Big Penguins

Emperor penguins are one of 18 kinds of penguin. All penguins are birds. Unlike most birds, however, penguins cannot fly. They stand straight and walk on legs that appear to be short but are mostly hidden by their feathers.

Here are three more big penguins.

King Penguin

The king penguin is the second tallest of all penguins. It can be up to 37 inches (94 cm) tall.

Gentoo Penguin

The gentoo penguin can be up to 35 inches (89 cm) tall.

Chinstrap Penguin

The chinstrap penguin can be up to 30 inches (76 cm) tall.

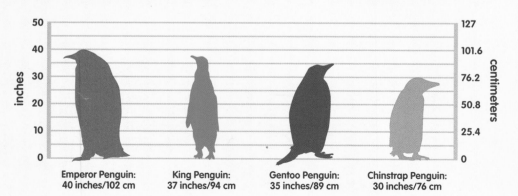

Emperor Penguin: 40 inches/102 cm

King Penguin: 37 inches/94 cm

Gentoo Penguin: 35 inches/89 cm

Chinstrap Penguin: 30 inches/76 cm

Glossary

huddle
(HUHD-uhl)
a group of
penguins crowded
close together to
stay warm

rookery
(RUK-ur-ee)
a place where
large numbers of
penguins gather to
mate

mate (MATE)
to come together
to produce young

waddle
(WAHD-uhl)
to walk awkwardly,
taking small steps
and swaying from
side to side

Index

Read More

Edwards, Roberta. *Emperor Penguins*. New York: Grosset & Dunlap (2007).

Jenkins, Martin. *The Emperor's Egg*. Cambridge, MA: Candlewick Press (1999).

Markle, Sandra. *A Mother's Journey*. Watertown, MA: Charlesbridge (2005).

Learn More Online

To learn more about emperor penguins, visit
www.bearportpublishing.com/MoreSuperSized